THIS SIDE OF THE FIRE

JONATHAN MAULE

AN INLANDIA INSTITUTE PUBLICATION

RIVERSIDE, CALIFORNIA

This Side of the Fire
Copyright © 2022 by Jonathan Maule

ISBN: 978-1-955969-07-9 (paperback)
ISBN: 978-1-955969-09-3 (ebook)

Cover art: L.I. Henley
Book design and layout: Mark Givens
Printed and bound in the United States
Distributed by Ingram

Library of Congress Cataloging-in-Publication Data

Names: Maule, Jonathan, author.
Title: This side of the fire / Jonathan Maule.
Description: First edition. | Riverside, California : Inlandia Books,
  [2022] | Summary: "In Jonathan Maule's elegiac and breathtaking poems,
  the speaker interrogates the self and ghosts from a violent youth. We
  see the edges of the horizon, gray and brown from perturbances of
  distant fires. We know from his lyrical and spacious poems, the fire
  lines are precarious, and in the breath of a caesura, the spark of their
  hungers may leap into the places of calm. Knowing this, Maule's speaker
  attempts to reconcile with his own fires, yearning to read the winds of
  his past and seeking a way to calm the burning within. This is an
  extraordinary collection. OLIVER DE LA PAZ"-- Provided by publisher.
Identifiers: LCCN 2021060784 | ISBN 9781955969079 (paperback)
Subjects: LCGFT: Poetry.
Classification: LCC PS3613.A87395 T48 2022 | DDC 811/.6--dc23/eng/20220107
LC record available at https://lccn.loc.gov/2021060784

Published by Inlandia Institute
Riverside, California
www.InlandiaInstitute.org
First Edition

THIS SIDE OF THE FIRE

JONATHAN MAULE

ACKNOWLEDGMENTS

Grateful acknowledgment is made to *Spillway* for publishing "Dear Red: I am Piling Dead Oleanders."

Thank you to Jennifer K. Sweeney for all your support and encouragement. Thank you to all the faculty at the Rainier Writing Workshop, and especially to Rick Barot, Kevin Goodan, Greg Glazner, Marjorie Sandor, Geffrey Davis, Kevin Clark, Oliver de la Paz, and Lia Purpura. Thank you most of all to Lauren; you are the reason I write. And finally, to Red: may you find what you are looking for and tell me all about it.

CONTENTS

I

LETTERS TO RED

IN A DOCUMENTARY

Mountaineers cling to ropes during a whiteout   rising

through ice   and when someone falls   a body becomes

an impossible shrine   on earth and gone

at the same moment   these places we reference

with our words   rescue cannot be spoken and so

time becomes our mouthpiece   the young man wanting

a closer look at Yellowstone's boiling pools   dissolving while

his sister watched   My sister is alive   thirty

goes by Red   her hair dyed many times   fatigued to the cuticle

maybe thinking the tattoos   piercings   drugs   booze

will disappoint me   forgetting I had them first   I said I wasn't

her father   years later we danced at a punk show   but now I

dream her in a blue flower dress   a freshman smiling in a state school hoodie

a rescued owl with one eye walking its cage   I ask her to sit and tell me

what threw her years into a single word   I see her

through the door of the blizzard   her foot rising

stepping through

DEAR RED

I can't see your face   so tell me
how does it change in a mirror?   Do you cook   and if so

have you found a way to shop for produce?   Do you check for cracks
in a dozen eggs?   Have you ever noticed the similarities

in our noses?   Prominent   people might say   I can't be sure
any of this will reach you

I couldn't see the stars   so I moved back to the desert
Each poem is a match I'm collecting for   what

a handful of smoke?   As you read this
there is music playing   even in the ocean of outer space

love and misery and rock 'n' roll   sparking from a golden record
casting simple messages into darkness   a way home

DEAR RED

Awake at four a.m.   sprawling a futon
the corner of a dark room

a mayfly pumping air into paper wings
no clocks   only the drapes

stand against the day
a rash of red desert

Awake at midday   a mirage in the mirror
acrid breath   she draws the drapes

the buildings   stripped of shadows
through the glass of the twenty-seventh floor

she holds up her fist
blocks out casinos with her thumb

eats from a plate of chocolate strawberries
leaving little green toupees bound to a gash of red

she wants a man to see her as a stuck ruby
something to labor over

the subject of a singular focus   strung up and
carved with a surgeon's touch

laid bare in the sun
the knives   rinsed clean

DEAR RED

Have you ever felt like all your ideas were porcelain dolls with big stupid heads
stacked on a crummy shelf in some rest home

senility wafting like a zephyr?   Maybe what you need is a funny poem
harmless and innocent as a baby giraffe

something fortifying   something you can put in your shoe
something toothed to prick yourself dream-proof   are you awake?

For example   are you aware that the most powerful man in the world
is a dirt-throwing ape?   OK   so this guy walks into a bar

sits   asks the bartender   *Have you ever witnessed the death of your ego?*
a complete oyster-shuck detachment of self?   Bartender looks at the man

says   *Sure   after work I pull myself out through my eyeballs*
hang big fat me on the coat rack inside my front door   drives the cat insane

If you wanted   this could all be a joke   Did you hear the one
about the baby with blown-glass eyes entering a push-up contest

winning a stack of flap-jacks taller than himself   seeing a future in it
becoming a diabetic   or the lion that caught a mouse

who begged for life   but was eaten anyway   Let's take
a picture of our faces first thing every morning   for six months

put all the pictures in a flip-book   call it *Floorin' it Through Life*
read it backwards   I still haven't heard from you

maybe my letters are too dull   up to their eyes in looking back
Think hard about the last thing we agreed on   see that's funny right there

was it more or less   than the last thing
we disagreed about?

DEAR RED

Is there a memory of us laughing I can borrow
hold to my ear?   Were we rolling?   Was it even funny?

Did we glimpse our time running thin   and just give in to
the sounds in our throats?

Did you ever hear me lose something profound?
A portrait?   An explanation?   Can you return it?

Will you read me the story of the past decade?
I'll keep quiet   make us tea   hold my questions

I'd like to tell you I've learned to use language   that I've been
spending my time helping people use it   but the fact is

I know as much about these words as I do ants   or tiger dentistry
which is to say   I'm simply mouth-making-a-donut amazed

I made it to thirty-five without falling into an open manhole
robbing a restaurant   moving to Denmark

which is to say   I've finally tried to be good
There was a small dog I rescued

scruffy and trusting   dug under the fence
devoured by coyotes anyway

Do you ever feel yourself speeding toward an unscenic ravine
thick with scrub brush   overgrown with heaps of smashed cars?

I'll be the big brother here   and remind you to
be kind to yourself   and others   if you can

buckle in   let the wind make
a flailing anemone of your hair

make what sense you can   and know I'll see
you at the bottom

DEAR RED

At the landfill   poking through the ruins
go back: this sliver of trash was perhaps a jug

carrying milk in its breast like a waiting mother
and further: plastic beads   sweating

losing their shape in a pot of polyethylene soup
go further: how much we owe to ancient bodies

to dinosaurs and the burning
engine of fossils

The men in tractors don't care for me   I know
there are signs about what I'm doing

but the doll hands keep waving me over   the burst refrigerators
look somehow sexual   wide open in the dirt

What is this lamp with no bulb?   Statue?
Homage to shadows?   The immortality of mirrors

still catching light   even when
the body is a bed of broken teeth

I convince myself that photos   lying in dog bowls
crushed under tires   have copies somewhere

siblings across town or
in a big city

The sun's rays   bouncing from a satellite dish
warming a pile of vegetables

I convince myself that
you are safe

that everything abandoned
is kin

DEAR RED

Staring flat a corner of desert   I caught a cactus wren falling
to the spiked mace of a cholla   carving from the air its descent

landing among the needles   plucking a song from the thorns
singing from a razored fist   above the riveted body

of an impaled lizard   stuck in a jump   the bird   flitting away
leaving each spine humming

There was a time I felt it would be better to stop breathing   just billow
and fold like an unmanned parachute   or make a penitent walk

into the mouth of a moonlit breaker   the only thing saving me being
more life and the hope for beautiful women   both of which I received

both of which I squandered   Little sister   what do you imagine
when you imagine death?   How are you navigating this heat wave we're in

Do you carry napkins for blistering doorknobs?   Do you sleep to the sound of
a fan spinning the air?   I wanted to ask   one desert dweller to another

are you getting enough water?   Do you see what's happening to the sun?
Is it just me or   as I write this   are we closer than we've ever been?

DEAR RED

The eye is a drunken jailor   falling asleep with the cages open
the memories of one cell   walk to the bunk of another

the mind screaming down the halls   jangling the eye's
massive key ring

Yesterday   a man shot from a hotel window   scattered
boots and blood in Vegas   from the thirty-second floor

the bullets fell like rain through music   through
more corpses and grass   plastic beer cups   straw hats

the undying light of the strip nearby   Today people line up
to donate blood   to pour themselves into the wounded

some say to pray   we are all just trying to make a body
feel more like a person

The eye is not a drunken jailor   my mind is not a cage
I can render you here   or in the Cayman Islands

cleaning a hurricane   bringing water to a child
or tucking bullets into the sleep of a magazine

singing country music   dancing in a hailstorm
If you were there   would you stand   mouth open

raindrop bursting
to meet your tongue?

DEAR RED

There is this lie I tell myself
while in one of those kinked hose kinds of moods

each word a thorn   or a bright electronic I crave
wanting so much to tell a story that is worth it

I want and want and beyond that
just a bag of guts taking up space and

later I am eating spaghetti when it occurs to me
that I could find you

it's only a city but
would I trade you being gone

for what I've written?
Is it the idea of you I write to

from here   where
through this window

I see my dog
walking the yard for something to chew

step on a goathead
and stand there   paw raised?

DEAR RED

There are no words for what animals must think of us   except
those squeezed from the vulture   crushed on the highway

a microcosm of our universe: the dead eaten by
the soon-to-be dead

If I could be an animal   I guess I'd be the ruthless one I am   watching
another cannibalized body on a plate of asphalt   becoming

an exclamation point to keep my dogs away from the street
The longer we go without talking   the more I augment

our last shared word   and the face   of whoever
spilled it   carelessly   as though

we had enough

DEAR RED

If what we forget says more
than what we remember

then we have said much
in our forgetting

each of us the dark spot
floating in the other's eye

a single blurred moment
drowning in a day—

on the stove   my silver kettle
spitting its insides over a spidered flame

or a bus   unclenching at the stop
gathering us as strangers

My memory has cataracts
a black sky pocked with glowing mouths

I stare right at them
I build you from these spaces

wait for you to speak
in the halls of our forgetting

something we can dance to
an offering

I never gave you   a digging tool
a mollusk   a wind-up kangaroo

a poem you may fold
into a star

DEAR RED

Yesterday I didn't think of you once and the wind
knocked around the cans in my yard

dusted glass shards I later tossed in a bucket
the dogs screamed at crows

chased jack rabbits   ate squirrel turds
offered their greedy bellies to the sun

Today a line of bloodstained chests wait to drink
from a swamp cooler downspout   their little heads

like the marbles I find in my yard after a storm   dipping and rising
threading droplets into the split seed of a beaked mouth   flitting away

and just like that you're here   standing in line with the birds
waiting for water and a chance to fly away

or is it toward   a desert unfurled by wind and coils of heat
where trash spills from truck beds

where Styrofoam disintegrates into toxic fish eggs
and each flayed ribbon of a tattered blue kiddie pool embraces

a cactus or fencerow   beer bottles and silver bullets
road sodas I once heard them called   ignored as every homeless body

heaped and huddled   somehow sacred
against the sky   crowned flechettes of Joshua Tree fists

the cradled orange of our moon
What are the odds these pieces would end up here   just now

below my feet   above my head   in my hand
piled in a yellow bucket?   What are the odds they'd end up anywhere else?

I don't see god out here or anywhere   which is to say I see more than
a silly man slapping the pieces of a broken train set

fixing everything to death   sand falling through fingers
I see the birthing

cycles of burrowing animals   find their jawbones
in holes tunneled under the house   the failed nests of doves

staccato dash of a rabbit   running   now pausing
carving a kind of stillness   her tense body

the color of sand and heat   and is it enough
to let what will   vanish

II

IDAHO

IDAHO

It's been years
but still feels right there and raw

I live in a desert now
write poems about how drunk

I used to be
how sober I am now

always looking over my shoulder at
the young men who raided golf courses

blew up mailboxes   said so many
stupid things to young women

Did you ever take time to study the ocean?
So perfect   the landlocked marine biologist

Reminds me of a poet I know
lives in the desert

We damn near killed ourselves back then
and sometimes I'm terrified

only one of us didn't make it
out of our twenties

S lived with an ache   something just outside and burning
remembered the combo but forgot the safe

I'm sorry for whatever made him
stick a pistol in his mouth and snap a picture

I'm sorry for the way we get what we ask for most
when we aren't that articulate

He said the kid was probably mine
said   *If it's got a big fucking head   I'm not paying child support*

He had that way of joking   like someone's life was driving fast
in the dark   clicking off the lights

I remember laughing at all those white houses
the living room couches and music videos

bright rooms with big beds
and a green cockatiel biting my cuticles

kitchens and the hands of fathers
dwarfing their coffee cups

gripping them the way
I tried to protect her

That other guy   when I called
wasn't scared   not at all

said he'd been recently stabbed
and maybe I'd give him a day or two before we fought

and when we cried
we cried together

After I headed west to play drums in a rock band
I know something broke between us

Was it S's death? Was it my words?
Anyway   we're all headed for more death and words

Here's a nod to the days we ran so fast
we couldn't tell the expressions on our faces

Terror? Joy?
Had enough?
Had enough?

THE WRESTLING COACH

Muscled thighs   wide as telephone poles   not many of us had seen

a man like that up close   and so   fear   jokes

wagers about the limits of his strength   I could do push-ups and pull-ups

run a quick enough mile   I had grown up with strong men

dressed in dark green flight suits   who seemed to sharpen their razors against

their jaw lines   I knew to not hang myself with my words

to not speak to these men unless it was their idea   But when my classmate

grew a tumor in her brain   coach took up a collection   shaved his head

wore a tutu over a singlet   complete with headgear   broke his thumb

wrestling a metal folding chair   for the amusement of the school

to raise money for the medical bills   and when my classmate died

coach kept his hair buzzed   kept teaching us how to sweep the knees

how to shoot in   tap out before your arm splinters

before your vision goes blurry   as black as sleep

WHAT IS EASY, WHAT IS HARD

Pulling a suckerfish from the stream

holding it on the bridge   Dad was waist-deep

I stared at the mouth   the blinkless eye   hated its suffering

couldn't unset the hook   bashed in its head with pliers

We couldn't have known   we thought of everything as swimming

toward us   I'm trying to get better at knowing what's better

left alone   how scrubbing those coins with toothpaste

as a child   dulled their copper faces

What yearning to shine a sock full of pennies   cleaning and loving

what holds my attention   to wipe clear

the blood   cast the slick body

under the bridge

FORT STREET

I.

The summer my father came home after flying
over oceans of Sitka spruce   looking for the black eyes

of oil leaks   he and I stripped the garage roof
tarpapered   re-shingled   dug a freshwater line

trenched with skinny shovels   swapped a hatchback's water pump
cut linoleum into the shape of a bathroom floor   lanced purple blisters

with a pin   soaked my hands in magnesium   I mowed and weeded
scooped cat shit from the tomato beds   sheared the rose bush

to a single flowerless stalk   then watched him fly away
a coin sinking into the well of the sky

Later   in the garage   I gathered ten plastic soldiers carrying rifles
grenades   radios   dowsed them

a snake of fire slithered back to the gas can
sounded like blowing out birthday candles

ten gallons of a slumped red jug   I threw water from a cat dish
the tangled umbilical of a hose

I knew my mother would recognize my burned body
the pink and blue slivers   the green and black pools

when he crackled through the phone   how I wanted to convince him
he was better than gold

II.

A list of what
I'm still grieving:

the violence
of a closed mind

the belt
fashioned into a noose

how shadow
defines light

In a family of seven
it is rare to be two

mother and son in the backyard
of a big white house

a moment floating
in a Boise summer

stretched across our picnic table
spotting falling stars

making a game of brevity
so full of crickets and night

After she is gone
may I hold the smallness of a picnic table

the fat and green of rhubarb leaves
the flash living in our eyes

the simple goal
of a shared star

something we could point to
Yes   I see it too

III.

I don't think video killed radio
I think radio killed itself   and we kept quiet about it

just kept on stealing music   forgetting the song for the ad
but surely   even now   there are children

pressing speakers to their heads   running scales or drilling rudiments
lured to the nourishment of sound   as the fingers give way to blood

I am always listening to the music of conversations
the intervals of a turn signal

Raised poor enough to know that true wealth
means no DJs roughshodding intros   it means the whole guitar solo

At ten   I'd steal cassettes to trap
the music we couldn't buy   all of which my mother

called *wicked*   and not in a good way
She sang hymns   stirred butter into macaroni

and   with the same wooden spoon
played me like a drum

BOISE HIGH

There was an afternoon   when three boys
skipped class

popped cans   lit kites to the air
from the middle of the track   a revolution of sugar and flight

to pilot their small power   laughing in public
their truancy from desks and neckties

joked about starting some kind of movement   how   after all
could a person do algebra in a prison yard

when the sun was tensing the skin
of plastic aircraft painted like a bird of prey

a space shuttle   an ice cream truck?   The air split open
when Buzz sauntered to the field

with his walkie-talkie   windshield sunglasses blazing
his stride and blue polo   everything screaming

the police department had not retired from him
Well, boys   it's a perfect day for deep shit

and Buzz stood   arms at his sides
eyes wandering the sky

under his bulletproof glasses   and   for a moment
getting caught was the point

four truants staring at the belly of an Idaho skyline
That one   what is it   an ice cream truck?

Give out some slack   let her breathe
let her breathe

WHAT IS EASY, WHAT IS HARD II

Film degrades as you view it
and memories don't fare much better

breath spreading algae across Paleolithic cave paintings in France
herds of charcoal horses   ibex   bison

As a widow   my grandmother sold her belongings
lived in a van she called *the turtle*

drove around the country
wrote a column for a newspaper

Later   convalescing and the smell of urine
her hair cut short and oily   the blue stones of her eyes

she spoke about my tattoo and a buffalo   the broken yolk of thought
made one small case against oblivion   as she looked through the window

What must those early painters have thought
harvesting minerals hundreds of miles away

trading a stone axe or spear for pigments
speaking the graffiti of their dreams to a mountain's guttyworks

like a jackknife saying to tree bark
despite everything   we were here

FAITH AND A SMALL GAME

The parking lot   ribboned with tar snakes

cloaked in the shadow of Saint John's cathedral

sits empty most days   save for three netless hoops

better than a milk crate nailed to a fence post

so I chip shots with a balding basketball

while the church bells sway like bats

On Sundays our parents take us to church

where white people sit like daisies

the drummer plays behind a plastic wall   draws me in

part of and apart from   and I want that kind of proximity

Years later   drumming in an abandoned Texas church

filling a room once punctuated by pews   with heavy metal

In the silence of a cathedral   still and empty as a hoop

what exactly were we practicing?

If you stand there long enough you may renounce your faith—

the only good church *is* an empty church   you might realize

or you might renew   If god ever spoke

how could we hear it?

The parking lot has a new fence now   a row of crocuses

the rich black surface radiates   the nets are new

they swish   sound better

than prayer

RED LIGHT AT 8TH AND STATE

It makes some sense   small talk
scraping our antennae   says

we are here   seen   I still do it but
always waiting to go home   next time

I'll ask   how many quarters can you fit in your mouth?
What is the shape of your throat?   I'll cut straight to it:

downtown opened like a butterfly knife
fermented green and red lights

someone punching expressions across my face
my drunk   the trees and mailboxes

all those fighting boys with fathers like brass rings
against the window

just strips of yellow light   opening a young man
a cage of ribs

all of us running   even when I won
what I did was worse than losing

one of us   struck on the back of the skull
blind   swinging at nothing

DIVISION STREET

And once   I met a girl's stepfather who   after we shook hands
showed me the gap where a hungry engine ate his ring finger

We sat on bald tires in a scrap yard   drank beers
talked about fistfights   the moment your head comes back online

you count your parts or slide a hand across your guts
admire the way it's all just an inch from the surface

Some nights were all hips and bong hits   cigarettes   little smirks ripped
in our jeans   driving golf balls against cars   pitching empties like sardines

to the parking lot's waiting mouth   nicotine and Dramamine
the myth of gravity

unemployment checks   food stamps   that split two-bedroom
a fur of cannabis and pills

The other couple kept a flying marsupial   with eyes like marbles
in a cage next to the bed   casually

as though everyone had a hunger like a beat-up pair of shoes
or a suspicious in-law

He said if I hurt her I'd never see it coming   only I never saw it anyway
just her fist one night screaming for me to fight back   *pussy*

I was the nose to her bullring   we were tires rolling downhill
waiting for someone   to break us apart

THE NORTH END

I cannot say why I thought to rob a car that day
Quick backseat bag snatch   a rummaging through the guts

to find college books and a portable CD player   which I kept
tossed the books in a blue dumpster   I'm sorry about it

but my head was a hive   I needed some daily break in
When I ran from the truck with pints of stolen cookie dough

there was nothing in me   shaped like an apology   Crime felt good
as nicotine or whiskey's hot snap   Fear was a city of wasps I ran through

toward the naked backs of broken glass minnows
silver in the sun

Fifth floor of a parking garage with a dud TV   size of a fridge
what final words would you think   as it tumbled out and down?

GOD'S MUSIC

The pews of the white Baptist church   dusted   polished

cupping the potted plant of each believer

When I played there   the music ran the risk of sin

careful not to shuffle   no backbeat   nothing in the shape of a gift

for women and their hips   Playing for the black Baptist church

the beat ushered believers into spirals of seizure flights   sprints to the stage

victory arms outstretched in fine suits and dresses   all our Sunday best

That little church   the uniform pleas of throats and hands   up-tempo

gospel rhythms spreading through the walls   through our chests

resonant chambers growing hot   Could I help it that   even without religion

something in that room spoke of faith   fellowship splashing

my eyes and shoulders?   When the church burned   we said

electrical   code   faulty   The rebuild   the gutted slab

regenerated into hallowed space   the workers saying nothing of the sacred

pouring a new building over the old good foundation

When it burned a second time   our eyes went out like candles

There are believers who'd rather not pray

than put their god in a box   and others

who eat their divinities

one slick piece at a time

THE PARTY

When I woke   everyone's eyes were switchblades

all glint and poke   scraping me to get on with it   the music

the rocks glass   hovering   full of wax   I tipped

into pills   out of doors

into rum   out of words

stairs shifting as I walked down   into summer

I wanted to freeze those people

freakish through my glass   I tried

all the words   I took off my face

passed it around   everyone took turns

smearing lipstick   crafting an ashtray

passing it on   was I asleep below

the anarchist saint on the roof   pouring beer

a crown of people gathered   but not

a single picture snapped   how the anointing must have

looked   spilling   the aluminum lip   falling

amber sheets   curling back

on my head

III

CALIFORNIA

GRACE AND FRANKLIN

When I show up to work with a splash of bird shit
tipping the black hill of my shoulder

my boss says I should be thankful   after all
what are the odds

Truth is whatever gets repeated   under the empty martini glasses
of these trees

I make lists and lists   walking these Hollywood tables
in my all-black get up   the Armenian chef   the French waiter

the muscular Native American bartender
b-list bingo nights   movie nights   nights against all fire codes

fighting upstream with trays of sloshing martinis   the porn star
giving me a hard time   her bodybuilder boyfriend mouthing an apology

the cocaine toilet   the sink ripped off the wall
nested in soggy white paper   My boss must think this is some luck

all these necessary bombs diving
from a sky heavy with gifts

Every scar is a story   the streak of pigeon shit on my chest
like some crooked insignia

our country   a pile of flags   a front yard littered with
inflatable candy canes

Maybe we should drink until the city rolls over for belly scratches
take a long drag off a bummed cigarette

What do you want to be
Siblings?   Friends?   Strangers?

When we board up the tiny windows of our eyes
something flies up

What are the odds it explodes with light above the lungs
of every burned-out club in America?

WILCOX STATION

In a jail cell   you fall into your stomach
it is the only motion

The walls   the floors   the eyes   locking shut
while a man screams for Jesus

I keep falling into this memory   as though the real
prison is trying to forget

Violence has a big mouth we crawl inside   baby crocodiles
smelling stomach acid and rust   peeking through tall teeth

There is a fat man   calls himself "Joker"   paces like a mad bear
his step   step   step   marking time

Across the hall   a man reclines on his bunk
with a copy of the Times

I want to leach his stillness   cool myself
against the marble slab of him

Suppose I thought of you then   in the falling
recognized my hands   balled into wrecking   making this cage

this ground floor   where locking eyes
leads further into a cellar

I walk my mind to a stone basin   to the idea of water
the food of a simple lie: we will be ok   we will be ok

OUR EYES JUST AS BIG

Stuck in Los Angeles   underground   then two towers

fish tanks crammed with nothing anybody wants

my body   other bodies   cattle   big stupid eyes

the walls   clubs   hosed-down cement floors

everything screams for space   people stand like this at concerts

or in line for tacos   the guard   big as a doorway   swings

a chunk of black steel   like his body was engineered for it

must have struggled in other jobs   snapping the femurs of massage clients

cannonballs heaved onto swimmers   I wonder when he discovered it

what the other kids must have said   I wonder how to foreshadow

a busted jaw   as in   baton   bursting into wet red verb

          as in   door   crashing

waiting is not the same as patience

TWIN TOWERS CORRECTIONAL FACILITY

In the sleepless pale light of
paper cut windows

each day a glowing cup of orange juice
and plastic food I do not eat

white as the slivered rib bone
stitched into the blue

of a young man's eye socket
in a hospital a few miles away

What does it mean
nothing but clothes and numbers?

It would take thirty-two years
to count to one billion and

forgetting is no small grace   especially now
brimming with corruption

I want drugs   I want the wrinkled flag
of a wrecked balloon

its yellow   held in the stray
wires of flight   thrashing a warning

or invitation   the same way
everything thrashes

when we need it still
as an answer

Above that steel bunk bed
I am a kite flying

over and over
against the walls

EMS

My brain is a spider
rolling silk over a sack of dreams
now wake and attend the screaming

boots on out the door at three a.m.
a child is seizing   he will live
now sleep

the word   *crash*   from Middle English
"to break into pieces"
now wake in boots

the man with a heart like old meat
will die under my hands
now sleep

the worst crashes   like the best bands
fast and loud   the young woman   burned her arms and breasts
now wake

the police officer   struck somehow by his own cruiser
now sleep   an ice climber   so close to rolling off
now wake

a grey blanket across her torso and she cries
now sleep   load the mother and daughter and baby
now wake

standing in the back   gripping a steel pole
now wake in the lights   wake in the sirens
wake in the crash

in the bodies bleached by overhead light   wake
the wheels have stopped spinning   the engines are dead
now sleep

the spider makes tight bundles
of the heart   the blood
the breath

THE BLUE LAKE CASINO

Walking the parking lot
more money from my car

my friend says the machines sound like paper shredders
a small bird flaps inside the tinted windows of a blue minivan

direct sunlight
windows up

When I was younger   I threw my insides out   the way a mollusk does
when it eats   The dishwasher in superheated grease

the cook in shining shrink-wrap   the waiter clinging like eggshell to black
plastic bags   the meatloader in freezers the size of stadiums

What to do with the inclination to keep things locked up
to have and to hold   zoos   museums   libraries for that matter

jails and prisons   where the lights are always shining
where even taking a shit is a gamble

there are no clocks   so time dies the way it does in a casino
in the never quiet   until the cell doors *cha-ching* like cash registers

spilling a violence of bodies   no one speaks except to wager
more and more   of what we have already lost

FIGHT OUTSIDE HOLLYWOOD PROPERTIES

And so I think of him
the young man
I nearly killed
fifteen years ago
I saw a promise on his face
but couldn't tell of what
and don't know if he is still wearing it
like a pair of sunglasses
or if he's had it
knocked away

We become so convinced
of ourselves
as though mirrors and pictures
offer proof
of what we are
all that's held up
the shaking lot of it
fragile as newborn mice

His boyish face
guttered with blood

How much of this
is life's beating
beginning
ending
easy as open your hand
close your hand?

MOVING IN

From the trash in my yard   shotgun-blasted sinks

murdered Christmas ornaments   music and furniture hauled outside

we cultivate a suspicion of fire and constellations   of grinning women pissing in

the lamplight   another oleander torched with butane

of men feeding the desert their empties and bottle-caps   their doorknobs and

broken butter knives   purple plastic eggs buried in tamarisk roots

burst fluorescent tubes flaking into burls   everything mimicking

the scattering of seeds

pulling a black rake through sand   piling what we can use and what

we must abandon   dropping glass teeth and chicken wire in a yellow bucket

the downed carcass of a power pole   sawing the arms and legs

off salt cedars for stove lengths   we bury cables and wrench a child's bed

from a dirt pile   next to the blown-out chicken coop

rinse my hands at the spigot   tend the burning of cactus

its blood smothering a flame   belching sweet smoke

from the same oil drum we found the curled bones of a juvenile dog

poured her into a plastic bag in the bed of a pickup   tomorrow

we will bury the fist of her rusted chain

THE MARINE CORPS AIR GROUND COMBAT CENTER

Standing at the front of a classroom
asking Marines to imagine their enemies

single-file them according to height
toes on a line   and then

just forgive them all
simple as washing laundry

or sweeping a floor
mindless as a chore

What if whatever we cannot say to one another
rhymes

and so our pain
is cousins at least?

What if fear and hate are simply ideas
like elbows or ice cubes?

Think melting
tired from bending

Could we drop a claw and snag
the worst in us by the scruff

or the dimpled skull
and simply yank it out?

What I know most
is hardest to love

HARMONY ROAD

I am piling dead oleander   mending
the crooked arms of my gate

that drag sand in and out   the way some children
make winter angels   their heated breath

cooling   dying
in the snowfall

Did you ever meet the Idaho gun-store clerk
the one with singed knuckle hairs?

Did you see the flash of light   from the clip
of his gut hook?

He would open glass cases   eject magazines and pull
back the slides   to show they were unloaded

Did a white price tag   cinched around the trigger guard
keep spinning   when he offered you the pistol?

I just want to say   this memory wears me
like a lead smock   Dough-necked men have poured

across this country   their cartoon gods
their unlimited guns

I just want to ask if you knew about that
gun-store clerk   about his house and

the cat in the freezer   what happened
to his children?

I had been there and never been there
I had seen them and never seen them

In the belly of that house   I felt the cold
in my chest   and kept quiet

It was all over the local news
that house   under a halo of helicopters

A DREAM OF GUNFIRE

The number of times you've been woken by gunfire says   what?

Could be downtown or scanning acreage

It means something too if you've never been the one at the trigger

just peering out   trying to catch the muzzle flash without losing something

you'll miss   Take Hollywood   the night after we carry a

sidewalk couch back to our apartment   we wake to a helicopter

and god's swinging eyeball   the spot-lit streets   man running

shooting over his shoulder   Those times a gunshot fooled your dreams

into a backfire   how the mind folds experience into a blanket

draped across the wrong mattress   I heard a shotgun this morning and assumed

it was my dog   which made me question   how is my dog a shotgun?

Her tail wallops   she's all trigger finger   if she were two words

she'd be *double barreled*   The sound drew me outside

where I used binoculars to spy on my neighbors

I want to say something useful about guns or dreams

firing image after image   but all I see is an orange blur

blowing craters   moving off   falling silent

What does it mean   that I never know

where the shooting is coming from?

THE MARINE CORPS AIR GROUND COMBAT CENTER II

Today the Marines
are in their costumes
and I
am in mine

bored
with peacetime
they are counting
the reasons they joined up
greeting me with
a bright question:

what should we argue about today?

I want to say
that a millionaire cowboy
singing about field labor
rings sour

that we all crave
the sound of our own voice
our own thoughts
we seek reflection and go home

a quiet young man
in the back
eyeballing me
as I strip his country
like an ear of corn

Here is the food   and this
you should not eat

THE MARINE CORPS AIR GROUND COMBAT CENTER III

The Marines   practicing war   planting bombs
rifling music   playing bodies of sand

bullets make their beds in the elbow of a wash   a mortar spits
I imagine the arc   the rising   falling shell

blossoming into glass   the desert   a split jar
rattled windows for miles   the worn logo on god's gunnysack

full of language and blast   what is noteworthy
the constancy of change we wrestle   none of this is surprising

like the way we talk about weather
Right now sure is hotter/colder than not now

You know   I told a room of Marines that god was female
that the caverns   behind her eyes   pluck us like strings

our bodies   a thin soup of music   picture a cold slab
picture marble   or granite the color of sand and blood

God is a quarry of bodies and wind   nibbling the bread of history
but what if god were suddenly a screaming child   impossibly fragile

a chicken's egg or a paper crane   in our pockets
next to a grenade?

LANGUAGE

I.

After the belly of another summer has taken its share

the bugs and their searching disappear

along with hot ribbons of sound from passing cars

the rubber on asphalt cooled   shoulders relaxed and open

all these nouns no longer busied by their verbs   We say cause and effect

casually handling our words   cheap as plastic frogs

press their backs and they will jump   I asked a dozen Marines

why we toss around language like   *god bless you*   why

if healing is our line of work   don't we abandon everything right now and

get to blessing   healing like mad the rising tide of the broken and the sick?

They must think I'm damaged goods   lost in the page's white space

I can see how the shine of my twenties was really a grease spot

But that's not it   at least   not precisely   I am simply amazed

at the cages   The next time I'm arrested   may it be for corrupting the youth

may a young man see himself without flinching   and may language rain

into the water table of my ear   unlocking me

II.

There is enough firewood   so we warm the belly of the house

stew knucklebones in the black Crock-Pot   read poetry

wear jackets and thick boots   watch the moon while our breath

leads us in loops around the property   Later   spring glides

drunk on life   Rain cleans the bald head of a gourd

and the earth drinks   Beneath our feet   water sits in taproots

a cathedral of egg shacks   glowing   so much waiting

to break free

III.

I look to the calendar's final ideas of one year   Winter makes

a living thing of me   I don't mean to say I'm dead and dragged

dashing my head against the coffee tables of other seasons

just that winter demands I be me again   To see the tree

as a source of heat   and gather it   to see my breath   to know the cold and

reckon with it   the air and the moon's empty face

the glorious dose of a new year's stupidity we dissolve on our tongues

as though the coyotes have lost our scent

I STILL LIKE SETTING FIRES

after Richard Hugo

I can still hear the M-80s of my adolescence
blasting craters at Camel's Back Park
the report of a dry-ice bomb
concussing the Treasure Valley

All those bombings and fake IDs
conveyor belts loaded with beer

What is it that makes a boy want to destroy a thing entirely?
Other boys   I suspect

I lost those friends   years ago
after a move to Hollywood   I must have seemed austere
or maybe we resent people who strike out blindly
with high hopes and a sack of clothes

Whatever it was   I was outside   they couldn't smell the gunpowder
on my fingernails   or I'd licked it away

I still like setting fires and blasting music   but I suspect
I've read myself into obscurity

Now, I hear Marines blowing shit up
and worry about their fingers   wonder how long until
they throw new fire at the sky

HAVE YOU SEEN THIS MAN

who lives like a ghost town
taking in weeds and beggars
whittling time through a crack in the door

the fulcrum of a weathered forearm
pulling down a jug from the high shelf
pitching a glug down to the gullet

not much for food or language
holes bug-chewed and leaking
a gust could scatter him like smoke

holding the shot glass sideways
looking through its telescope
at everything bulging and wet

the face of his boots
wilted into white chairs
folded down at the end of a wedding?

THE EPISTEMOLOGY OF SNAKES

after Geffrey Davis

Tonight the moon is huge and red
L and I are wearing heavy boots

waiting for our dogs to urinate   but
they are sniffing   staring beyond

our lights   at the shadows of what
has fallen   scattered like bones

the city below our feet
each black beetle   a drop of wet tar

raising its ass in silent warning
the body as weapon

not unlike the curled snake I found
beneath my gate one evening   a green

twist of muscle punctuated
with a flat of brown diamonds

stacked tail of clattering plates
tongue painting my silhouette   just

a juvenile   and yet   more dangerous
the smallness of a child's fingers

tracing gunmetal in his mother's purse
I walked under the sky's amethyst bowl

to the flat-nosed shovel
leaning against the shed

Coming home the next day   I found
the headless body   wriggled free

from the burial   one final gesture   as though death had
remade itself   as sand and heat   the sun itself

IV

CODA

SEATTLE WITH L

The museum and garden spilling with butterflies   eyes on their wings

a tour of planets   a laser show   sheep brains held in our hands

rooms of glass   hard candies for giants   lights from our flashes

bouncing from chandeliers   and here   a milk white eel climbing

glass bamboo   homage to its living counterpart across town

At the aquarium   cuttlefish huddle in shifting ranks   a portal rises

from the floor swelling with jellyfish   the city spools out

we order fat steaks   walk to the harbor   the sun and cochineal sky

smoke and clouds rendered by a burning forest   each curling flame

shot through with orchestral violence   After sundown

we ride the Ferris wheel   just this side of the fire   forgotten

on a giant spinning machine   watching a city tuck in while the lights

slide into sound   May every turning chamber be one we share

ABOUT THE AUTHOR

A graduate of the Rainier Writing Workshop, Jonathan Maule's first book of poetry, *Dog Star*, was published by Big Yes Press, and his written work has also appeared in *Askew, Talking River, Rain Taxi, RHINO Reviews!, Spillway*, and *Phoebe*. Jonathan's music, *Electric Mullet Sound Bath Experience*, is available to stream online. He lives in the high desert with his partner, writer and visual artist L.I. Henley. www.jonathanmaule.com

ABOUT INLANDIA INSTITUTE

Inlandia Institute is a regional non-profit and literary center. We seek to bring focus to the richness of the literary enterprise that has existed in this region for ages. The mission of the Inlandia Institute is to recognize, support, and expand literary activity in all of its forms in Inland Southern California by publishing books and sponsoring programs that deepen people's awareness, understanding, and appreciation of this unique, complex and creatively vibrant region.

The Institute publishes books, presents free public literary and cultural programming, provides in-school and after school enrichment programs for children and youth, holds free creative writing workshops for teens and adults, and boot camp intensives. In addition, every two years, the Inlandia Institute appoints a distinguished jury panel from outside of the region to name an Inlandia Literary Laureate who serves as an ambassador for the Inlandia Institute, promoting literature, creative literacy, and community. Laureates to date include Susan Straight (2010-2012), Gayle Brandeis (2012-2014), Juan Delgado (2014-2016), Nikia Chaney (2016-2018), and Rachelle Cruz (2018-2020).

To learn more about the Inlandia Institute, please visit our website at www.InlandiaInstitute.org.

ABOUT THE HILLARY GRAVENDYK PRIZE

The Hillary Gravendyk Prize is an open poetry book competition published by Inlandia Institute for all writers regardless of the number of previously published poetry collections.

HILLARY GRAVENDYK (1979-2014) was a beloved poet living and teaching in Southern California's "Inland Empire" region. She wrote the acclaimed poetry book, *HARM* from Omnidawn Publishing (2012) and the posthumoussly published *The Soluble Hour* (Omnidawn, 2017) and *Unlikely Conditions* (1913 Press, 2017, with Cynthia Arrieu-King) as well as the poetry chapbook *The Naturalist* (Anchiote Press, 2008). A native of Washington State, she was an admired Assistant Professor of English at Pomona College in Claremont, CA. Her poetry has appeared widely in journals such as *American Letters & Commentary, The Bellingham Review, The Colorado Review, The Eleventh Muse, Fourteen Hills, MARY, 1913: A Journal of Forms, Octopus Magazine, Tarpaulin Sky and Sugar House Review.* She was awarded a 2015 Pushcart Prize for her poem "Your Ghost," which appeared in the Pushcart Prize Anthology. She leaves behind many devoted colleagues, friends, family and beautiful poems. Hillary Gravendyk passed away on May 10, 2014 after a long illness. This contest has been established in her memory.

OTHER HILLARY GRAVENDYK PRIZE BOOKS

among the enemies by Michael Samra
Winner of the 2020 Regional Hillary Gravendyk Prize

The Silk the Moths Ignore by Bronwen Tate
Winner of the 2019 National Hillary Gravendyk Prize

Remyth: A Postmodern Ritual by Adam D. Martinez
Winner of the 2019 Regional Hillary Gravendyk Prize

All the Emergency-Type Structures by Elizabeth Cantwell
Winner of the 2018 Regional Hillary Gravendyk Prize

Our Bruises Kept Singing Purple by Malcolm Friend
Winner of the 2017 National Hillary Gravendyk Prize

Traces of a Fifth Column by Marco Maisto
Winner of the 2016 National Hillary Gravendyk Prize

God's Will for Monsters by Rachelle Cruz
Winner of the 2016 Regional Hillary Gravendyk Prize
Winner of a 2018 American Book Award

Map of an Onion by Kenji C. Liu
Winner of the 2015 National Hillary Gravendyk Prize

All Things Lose Thousands of Times by Angela Peñaredondo
Winner of the 2015 Regional Hillary Gravendyk Prize